Skipping Rocks at High Tide

The Poetry of Joshua Lorenzo

PublishAmerica
Baltimore

ISBN: 1-4241-3428-5
PUBLISHED BY PUBLISHAMERICA, LLLP
www.publishamerica.com
Baltimore

Printed in the United States of America

This book is for my wife Stacey and my daughter Abby. May we continue down the road of life together.

Table of Contents

Love   7 — 16
Heartache   17 — 29
Fatherhood   30 — 34
Death & Dying   35 — 45
Seasons   46 — 48
Anger   49 — 56
Goodbyes   57 — 67
Current Events   68 — 69
Life & Aging   70 — 86
Competition   87 — 91

Inaction Is Action

Fall, 2001

In my imagination you and I danced many of my insecurities away.
But no matter how much fun we had, you were never there the next day.
That damn front door always closed with you on the other side.
No matter how much poetry I recited or how many tears you cried.
No amount of evening walks changed a thing. You always found your car.
And I hated those awkward goodbyes because inevitably the silence took me too far.
Eventually I learned to move past the occasions to feel vulnerable, trying to endure the pain.
But I always endured it alone, getting soaked by a drenching rain.
I watched myself in those evening puddles, floating around in the drink that never ends.
As I wondered for many hours if there were any rules that I could bend.
But as time passed by and the coffin of our time was placed into the ground.
I realized that my inaction is what saved me before I drowned.
Those unanswered prayers I was mad at God for not addressing,
Turned out to be, in a few years time, the biggest of all blessings.
Sometimes it is our inaction that helps us find our way through the foggy haze.
I was stuck in many moments I never thought I would get out of, but I found those better days.

Similar Journeys
Summer, 1999

It isn't the fact that you are currently involved.
What scares me is the fact that my hopes have evolved.
I hope for realities that always appear to be faked.
And that this whole world will change for one mans sake.
If I only see things as black or white, and I always appear blue;
And you always smile, what color does that make you?
Do you change your position to make yourself smile?
As honestly as you admit that, are you still in denial?
I try to shake up my own life to keep it less stagnant;
Then hold onto hope and strangle it like a magnet.
Are these actions a result of what I say or what I hear?
Because I know I have tried whispering thoughts into your ear.
Will the solution to this problem ever be heard?
Or is this simply a recipe that doesn't have to be stirred?
I can no longer throw stones into the sea and hope that they float;
Nor can I pretend to be Shakespeare, reciting his quotes.

Highs & Lows

Winter, 2000

Retrospectively, life is short. It is full of moments we all add drops of sugar to.
Memories are full of wonderful times that in the moment may have left us blue.
It seems true that when things are going well, they never seem to last that long;
But it seems impossible to control the tailspin when things start going wrong.
Sometimes it seems like steering is lost, tires are flat and the brakes are out of juice;
And the accident that follows is just God's way of letting things gets loose.
But yet at other times we seem to get by with luck and good looks, seemingly unshakable.
We watch from our thrones the throng of people who are vulnerable and breakable.
It isn't worth trying to make sense of either. How can you make sense out of disarray?
I have learned that neither lady luck nor the worst of luck are truly ever here to stay.
The grass is rarely greener on the other side. And even if it is, just enjoy the grass you see.
We seem to spend an awful lot of time trying to make people the way we would like them to be.
Let us just enjoy the time we've had and the time we have remaining.
Don't get too excited when the sun is shining or too depressed when it starts raining.

It's All Uphill

Fall, 2001

It isn't the fear of the unknown that scares me, it's the known coming to an end that does.

I seem to have spent an awful lot of time in my life, thinking about what was.

Can the backaches be from carrying the weight of the world on my shoulders?

The choice is either trudging uphill into fatigue or running downhill dodging boulders.

Why can't I just stop the madness in my mind for more than one day at a time?

I doubt God wanted me to be a constantly running train. When is giving up not a crime?

These bags under my eyes do not blind me from the world that I am meant to see.

They just collect the falling tears as I get up off the ground, dusting off my knees.

How can a glass be half full in the morning and almost empty as the sun begins to set?

Sometimes I feel like I am dodging drops of rain while fate is trying everything it can to get me wet.

I seem to search for the light switch on many nights, only to discover that the power has gone out.

And when I finally accept that I cannot see what is in front of me, I discover what my life is all about.

Coping with the situations that arise on one hand and trying to make them better on the other.

In the meantime leaning on the one who understands my evolution and perhaps that is why I love her.

My Future Wife

Fall, 2001

You have become a friend and a lover, someone that I can trust.
I love thinking back to all the things that we've discussed.

When the day seems long and tiring, I can think about your smile.
And with a renewed sense of vigor I can climb another mile.

I thank you for being you and all that you have shown.
I cannot put into words how the desire in my heart has grown.

I want to enjoy every moment with you, even if they go too fast.
With not even one guarantee in life, I feel in my heart that we will last.

So as we take it day by day, making new footprints in the sand.
Let us always be able to smile and laugh, walking hand in hand.

Love Is

Fall, 2001

Falling in love is like smelling a rose for the very first time;
Or hearing the voices to a beautiful song and almost anticipating the rhyme.
It is the overwhelming anticipation of seeing your loved one coming into view.
It is the ability of keeping your life in perspective, while keeping the relationship new.
It is a kiss from a lover you hardly ever thought you could find.
Through a world of disillusion, it is two people remaining kind.
It is the want and desire to freeze certain moments in time, hoping they remain clear.
It is the inevitability of losing each other that overwhelms the heart with appreciation and fear.
Being in love is protecting uncertain hearts from bouts of certain indecision.
It is sorting through the emotions, not always having understanding and precision.
It is falling for a person who has the capability of wounding your heart.
It is hoping the rewards outweigh the risks and that trust will do its part.
Falling in love is a verbal agreement between the heart and mind.
It is what two people have thought impossible to find.
It is wishing and praying that the individual will not be lost to the crowd.
It is a moment of clarity when those inner voices grow too loud.
It is the inside of a hurricane as the wind is whipping all around.
But in the center of destruction, two people do not hear a sound.
It is the ability to dance when the music ended long ago.
It is a feeling I have for you Stacey. I am unable to explain, I just know.

Goodbye
Spring, 2005

The trees are shedding their leaves as a tearful goodbye is growing more inevitable with each moment that passes.

All I seem to be left with are fleeting moments of July picnics spent laughing on summertime's grasses.

The morning mist rises up over the lake as it always does. The familiar chill is in this early autumn day.

And no matter how badly I yearn to keep you here with me, I know it is impossible for you to stay.

This feeling is like staring at an alarm clock two minutes before you know it will go off, ringing deafly in your ears.

I have nothing but the unending question in the front of my mind, "what happened to all of our years?"

It all comes down to one last touch of the cheek, knee deep in cold waters, as she begins to row away.

Two hearts breaking into a million pieces each as you baptize yourself in the water, unable to Pray.

Wishing that the tides would take you with her or the currents would take you under.

That God would get so mad at the scenario he would burn the lake and throw down thunder.

But nothing makes a sound except a bird, searching fervently for a meal from last night's rain.

He, like every other living thing, seems absolutely impervious to my pain.

And as her last image disappears into the afterlife, I find myself sitting numbly on the bank.

I am alone for the first time since I can remember, with no one to blame for my sorrow and no one to thank.

This time, the alarm going off rings into my ear and I am thankful for the realization of a dream.

And the reminder that no matter how badly things may look at a given moment, they are better than they seem.

Bonds That Go Unspoken

Summer, 2003

You are everything I could have hoped for. You make the most wonderful wife.

Despite my certain inaccuracies, I hope you will always be a part of my life.

Sometimes the road ahead becomes distorted by the fog of everyday trouble.

Your version of happiness is superb and I hope I never burst your bubble.

We may see things differently and we will handle them as such.

No matter what, my heart will melt at the very hint of your kind touch.

Sometimes my life becomes confusing by outside forces that are pulling me down.

But with you as my life jacket, I know that I will never drown.

In the end, all that will be left is what we created all those years ago.

Two seeds being given a lifetime to establish ourselves and grow.

That is the beauty of what we are making. There will be bumps along the way.

I will make mistakes by what I do and do not say.

But no matter what, it is you and I. It is a bond between two people that will never be broken.

The love that we have made together is a bond that isn't even spoken.

Head's up Together

Summer, 1998

Could you let me see what is causing you pain?
I yearn to be your jacket when the tears fall down like rain.
Let me be the one to hold you when you start shivering in fear.
The lonely cold can never touch you as long as I am near.
Show me that smile and sweetness from your lips.
My kiss could be the tea that warms you with each sip.
May I touch your fragile shoulder when the night turns bleak and cold?
I want to stare into your eyes forever and watch ourselves grow old.
Would you let me hold onto your hand and lead you to forever?
Hand in hand we walk into sweetness, heads up and together.

Morals
Winter, 1998

Can a moralistic man find a woman who sees,
that you don't always have to bring a man to his knees?
When the words of your voice come out tried and true,
does it make you feel better to make me feel blue?
When you speak of the future are you clutching your heart?
or clenching your fists, laughing as it all falls apart?
It is not new to me, I have seen this before.
The opportunity dies and you slam the door.
You may wonder for a moment and see a man from the past,
But quickly become preoccupied with events that will make him fade fast.
You may even have known that the man in your life,
Was ultimately the blade of a very dull knife.
Perhaps instinct told you that you just wanted to have fun.
And that very same instinct said we were done.
So time will tick by as I wait for your call,
And do damage control as I wait for the fall.

Friends

Fall, 1998

There she stood with that wonderful, guilty grin.
My heart skipped a beat as I welcomed her in.
She continued to smile while I continued to fear,
What the devil was whispering into my ear.
Her eyes were like emeralds in the warm month of May.
The little devil on my shoulder asked me to ask her to stay.
She was sinfully guilty and yet innocently demure.
And for the heartaches I had known, I knew she was the cure.
We walked for an hour as the heavens led the way.
The stars were like vacuums that pulled my blues away.
She looked so strong and steadfast in the way that she walked,
And I felt her emotions pour out when she talked.
We ended the journey as we stood by her car.
And while the night was terrific, we stood apart too far.
Between the feelings we shared and the emotions I had,
When she left for her boyfriends, it left me quite sad.

Letting Go
Winter, 1998

Would it be a mistake to let her know how I feel?
When my heart is on the shelf, available for her to steal.
I cannot seem to get her off of my mind,
And the tunnel vision sight of her is making me blind.
I want to tell everyone I know what this woman means to me.
But the situation is such that I cannot reveal what I now see.
We have walked and talked together, danced my imagination away.
But it always ended with a goodbye because she could never stay.
And it doesn't help when all I want is to see her so much.
I just want to run and jump into her soft, secure touch.
That won't happen though and painfully I know it to be true.
It is better for me to zip my lip and pretend she does not have a clue.
And move on past this occasion to feel vulnerable while learning to endure the pain.
I will continue to stand alone on a path of isolation, getting drenched by the rain.

Heights
Spring, 1997

I climbed the rainbow yesterday afternoon when the sky was still black and blue.

I was working hard to overcome my fear of heights because I so badly wanted to look at you.

Then I found the tallest tree on this planet and began climbing up, looking for your face.

But all I could find were branches and birds wondering what in the world I was doing in this place.

So then I charted a plane whose pilot was the biggest risk taker of them all.

But he cowered out at a certain elevation because I guess he was afraid of the fall.

Then I found the biggest Ferris wheel in the world and at the highest point I reached out.

But that failed too and in frustration and disappointment, I began to curse out loud and carry about.

I was finally able to stowaway on a space flight that took me quickly to the stars.

But we must have overshot Heaven because we ended up on Mars.

At that point in my quest I began to realize that a memory would be all that I could carry.

And that I won't be able to see your face again in this lifetime and that proposition is somewhat scary.

Naked Trees

Summer, 2001

The naked trees have all but shed their leaves for the unknown paths that lie ahead.
While empty souls nurse the hangovers of the yesterdays still inside their heads.
The final nail in reality's coffin has been hammered in today.
Nothing normal remains from what we knew, it just simply went away.
Tears were shed from falling eyes, leaving stains on the summer grass.
We hold on for one more touch before this chapter comes to pass.
The stream is meeting the river and the river is meeting the sea.
And you head off to another start that won't be involving me.
I never took the time to notice how truly far apart we weren't.
So you need to understand how much saying goodbye to you really hurts.
My eyes are raw with emotion and nothing is what it seems.
The old man in my soul is crying while the young boy wants to scream.
I just saw the last train full of comfortable strangers leave with faint smiles and warm receptions.
All that seems to be left of me now are the sorrowful lovers and their indiscreet deceptions.
What used to be so wonderful has faded, in search of those gloomier days.
It feels as if the sand and the ocean have broken up and parted ways.
It is as if the stars shine during the day and the sun wakes up at night.
Or the goodhearted people break the law and the criminals set things right.
It is as if the trees have no leaves and all the grass is turning blue.
Constant confusion is the end result of what your departing actions will do.
Only one thing remains a constant, the hands on the clock will continue to tick.
It is a very faint reminder that time will eventually heal everything that makes me sick.

Headlines

Summer, 2001

I guess I saw the headlines from across the great divide.
You and I were on the same path, just looking for different rides.
I can try my best to be a contestant in your game, but that just isn't fair.
And it really isn't nice of you to expect me not to care.
I may fall fast and I may fall hard, but I will get up once more.
You only get one, maybe two chances to knock on my opportunistic door.
I may feel things in life with more impact than a lot of other guys.
Call me a professor of false potential or a listener of lies.
Feelings are not like a yard sale these days and I have never been a seller.
Nor am I going to dance around on eggshells when I have something I need
to tell her.
I can walk hand in hand with you as long as I have permission.
But I truly feel the cancer between us will never see remission.
What I have to do right now is simply disappear.
You no longer have to look to the sky in disgust when I speak into your ear.
Call it a learning experience that fell faster than a shooting star.
Just don't give me that look of regret. Simply get into your car.
Perhaps when I just go away you will find that we were right.
But I won't hold onto that lonely thought. At least I won't tonight.
There has got to be something out there for me, across this great divide.
In the meantime I need to look at what I am capable of from the inside.
I will do this right as I feel I have done before.
Placing the band aid on the wound and then learning from the scar.
Ultimately you choose your fate and right now I must start choosing mine.
Life's roads can treat you well if you take the time to read the signs.

Beaches of Life

Summer, 1998

The sun fell down beyond the waves of the sea,
While the last hint of yellow brought your memory to me.
Footprints where I have been, placed firmly in the ground.
And in front there is nothing, no footprints around.
Little girls innocently build a castle out of the wet hard sand.
A little boy finds destruction with the wrath of his hand.
His high pitched laugh was only temporary fun.
An overweight father glared strongly when he found out what his boy had done.
I just continued to march over the fresh hard grain,
Making prints in a life that has been all but plain.
The air that I ingested was salty and sweet,
And multiple towels lay together, empty and neat.
The rumble of the waves exuded the life they were willing to show.
And yet they fell silent as if they suddenly grew too afraid to grow.
Infinite possibilities in the ocean I saw,
But I still shed a tear for each wave that must fall.
Because the sea without waves, looks as if it always aches.
So it gives them another chance to learn from their mistakes.

Reinvention

Summer, 2001

It looks like I have averted another disaster I tried really hard to create.

Because it isn't always enough to simply have serenity on ones plate.

We drive lonely roads everyday, looking to invent an emotion that already exists.

And when we find it and are lured into it, we are frustrated the next day with what we could not resist.

I wish I had another sunset and a different set of circumstances sometimes, but you only have one life.

And you can't run from the choices you made just because regret yields its bloody knife.

So I broke into the amusement park again. The lure of the rides were enough to bring me back.

It has been years since I have feasted from the opportunity, and all I really wanted was a snack.

Or at least to window shop in search of something I will never really know.

Perhaps a renewed appreciation of what I have, or a feeling I put away so long ago.

Will Heaven Allow? (for an old friend)

Summer, 2005

The song playing is of no importance. The words are not making their way into my head.

I just float like a skipping rock on a pond, worrying about what to say and what was said.

With a sweaty right hand on her lacey back, we rotate like an anxious carousel.

Catching quick gazes into each others eyes, I fish for a story that I hope she will tell.

Befuddled by a strange beauty in front of me, I pray that Heaven will be as serene.

But a four minute song will not get a stranger to know completely what I am trying to mean.

The subtle clichés are flowing like a cheap country wine, the song starts hitting its peak.

There is nothing worse than a grown man struggling simply to speak.

The other couples dance as effortlessly as a morning spring breeze in constant domination.

But all I have brought with me is a heavy heart, teary eyes and a lot of hesitation.

What I feel is a prayer answered just a couple of years too late. Timing is a real sharp dagger.

And I am the bloody victim stumbling away from the dance floor, almost drunk with sorrow as I stagger.

No one else can see my pain, either they don't really notice or they never really cared.

I just wonder why my ego always stomps my appreciation and that fact makes me scared.

And as I look at her once more I find a brief period of salvation, a tender and subtle goodbye.

With that I am left with my arms extended in willing acceptance, looking towards the sky.

But I manage one more smile of innocence before letting go of her strange lacey scent.

I think I finally understand the importance of my mortgage at home, even if at times I want to rent.

With the last note hitting a low flat key, I wipe the sweat from my furrowed brow.

And I sprint back to the life I intend to keep, if only Heaven would allow.

Voids

Summer, 2000

I know that you will no longer be here to finish what I was always unable to start.
And frankly, that is the void in my soul that is ultimately breaking us apart.
I thought about it in depth over the last few days and I have come to accept the defeat.
I was proud to admit that I was able to keep my crushed feelings discreet.
I do find it hard getting over what I never took the time to know.
Those types of shortcomings make it impossible for me to grow.
Now I have visions of empty promises and even emptier chairs.
I always look to strangers for comfort despite the fact that no one cares.
I always had the opportunity to explore the things I didn't understand, but I never had the strength.
The only mistake I didn't make was being blind and following you at length.
I wanted to tell you the story, long before you left. I just never had the chance.
Now I sit here wishing the band would have played us one more dance.
But the ballroom floor is empty as couples have matched their seeking hearts.
I hold my head in between my hands, watching my soul crumble into parts.
There was an undesirable image of what I thought you wanted me to see.
If I had the chance to take it all back, you would know that was not me.

Seller of Goodbyes
Spring, 1998

No more lonely tears flowing out of lonely eyes.
There are only naked sidewalk sales, selling their goodbyes.
No more broken promises, no more absent nights.
There are only inner demons promoting one man fights.
No more cloudy systems that are passing overhead.
There are only empty pillows on an unmade stretch of bed.
No more wasted efforts, or lonely nighttime talks.
There are only empty promises and lonely nighttime walks.

Sometimes

Fall, 1998

Sometimes you cannot help a person, who is engulfed in their own pain,
Even if you desire to be the umbrella that would protect them from the rain.
Sometimes she has to cry to soothe her burning, tired eyes.
You need to let her see that often times, even love lies.
Sometimes the best thing to do is to simply walk away.
We all remind our beating hearts that life will be okay.
Sometimes it is the separation that makes the ride so sweet.
What we do not learn in victory, we usually do in defeat.
We all must bump our heads. It is the only way to grow.
It is not always the finish that becomes important, so let us try and take it slow.
It seems we crave the fire, but we cheat to get the spark.
It isn't only little children who fear what they hear inside the dark.

To my Mommy

A poem for my Mom on Mother's Day, with help from my Dad.
Love, Abby (and Josh/dad)
Spring, 2005

Sorry I made you uncomfortable for nine months Mommy,
But I sure did enjoy my time swimming inside your tummy.
You and daddy gave me life and I will do my best too make you proud.
Please do not get upset with my wet diapers or when you think I cry too loud.
You did a good job with my new room as well. I really love my little chair.
And you are probably surprised by the lack of heartburn that I have all this hair!
We will be a nice little family. But I do hope one day we will get another kitty.
And I cannot wait to meet Grandma in North Carolina, or Uncle Johnny in the city.
All the Vandor's and the Goodman's will be around as well, making sure our lives are great.
Perhaps you and Aunt Vanessa can help Dad out when I am nervously awaiting my first date.
Grandma Debbie and Grandma Paula will be there for questions you may have regarding me.
And I will have so much fun with Grandpas Mike and David, playing horsey on their knee!
Erin and I will have fun being friends, and I will probably be better at math than my Dad.
But if I get his compassion and your appreciation for life, no matter what else I will be glad.
I just wanted to say happy Mother's Day to you and thanks for allowing me into your life.
You will make a wonderful mother because already you are a terrific woman and a beautiful wife.

My Son
Winter, 2001

Watch out my son for the bumpy rocks along the way.
Do not count on tomorrow fore it will soon be yesterday.
Temptations are all around, sneaking up on you from behind.
They sometimes are not what you are searching for but simply what you find.
Look out for the disillusion that will eventually take a hold of you.
It will surround your familiarity, making your heart bleed blue.
And just because the past has already occurred, does not mean it cannot teach.
Be hesitant of the advice you receive, but always practice what you preach.
Do not be afraid to test the boundaries that your society will create.
"Heartache" and "heartfelt" walk a fine line in life, but do not discount fate.
Pray for human nature to endure when you hear the nighttime sirens in your head.
Listen to the stories of the elder man passing and remember what he said.
Please son, do not repeat the things that I have done.
Do not be the one staring down the barrel of a gun.
Please son, do not look for the trouble that I have seen.
Life is not always about black and white, so learn the in between.

Dimly Lit

Spring, 2005

The dimly lit halls in the middle of the night beckon out to a ship that is lost at sea.

And no matter how many times I try to tell myself it isn't true, that damn ship is me.

I feel like the little child under his desk, wondering if the sirens indicate a real air raid.

Subconsciously wishing for the ability to blend in and walk on by with the passing parade.

A fugitive on the run from chaos I am, unable to keep my reddened eyes out of the light.

Knowing and not knowing how to accept what I won't understand tomorrow, tonight.

I am sour in my stomach, sour in my head and frightened all around.

Not able to stop my mind from running my body into the ground.

Fatigue based of the emotional kind brings out the fearful lion in us all.

I am afraid of making a mistake or even worse, not being able to stand up tall.

Tempers flare like volcanoes while wishes spring eternal in a vacant forest.

It is at these moments when my morale, invincibility and demeanor are at their poorest.

And then in the blink of an eye I have healed. Almost as if nothing were ever wrong.

I return to the place in my mentality where I was nurtured, able and strong.

And so goes parenthood after eleven days, filled with uncertainty and restoration.

Moments involved are as low as the lowest cave, or as high as the highest space station.

Roads

Winter, 2005

The roads I have traveled over thus far have been relatively straight and without danger.
Sure, I have treaded over some rough patches, hit some potholes and picked up strangers.
But it has been a self teaching journey, filled with scenic seas and luscious mountain tops.
A highway full of cruise control with only the bare minimum amount of red light stops.
But I get the feeling that the road ahead will be somewhat strange to me, never navigated before.
It is a somewhat unsettling feeling not having control, or even a hint of what might be in store.
Like knowing that the sun will set eventually and that nighttime will be out in full force.
Despite the darkened highways in the future, I know I need to remain steadfast and on course.
People are relying on me to make it to places perhaps their cars wouldn't allow them to travel.
I will try desperately to keep everything in perspective, before the traffic makes the mind unravel.
Just knowing that I will have others in the car with me is enough to keep me stretching for another mile.
And I am pretty confident that the people, who are too afraid to keep going, are stuck in a state of denial.
So with that I just keep the pedal down and the window open while the vague turns are coming into view.
And with a renewed sense of purpose I turn up the radio, understanding I have a long way to go before I am through.

Circular Optimism

Fall, 2004

The skies of uncertainty have passed us by, replaced with an electric blue.
The crossroads I have just skated over signify that my self doubt is through.
And I don't think there is a mountain I can't get over now, nothing is in my way.
As a matter of fact there isn't one damn thing that will pull me down today.
Perspective is being put into place right now. It will take many more months to show.
But I have no doubt that my optimism and outlook will continue to grow.
And the file cabinet in my mind that contains the doubt and worry is finally being locked.
Replaced with the marathons of happiness I plan on running, you can put us on the clock.
As the leaves will begin to fall this autumn, my spirits will begin to rise.
And the determination for what is truly important will be obvious in my eyes.
By the time next spring rolls around, a new man will have come out of my skin.
And the next chapter in the life of a rollercoaster will begin.

Gates (For Penny)

Summer, 2001

Well this is the end of my journey as the gates are just beyond those hills.
I can only now wish for the time back in my life that I have carelessly killed.
Will I be back to roam this earth? I only wish I knew.
There were so many things that I put off that I now wish I could do.
I guess you could say that at this point I have grown a little scared.
Not in the certainty of death but rather in the fear that no one really cared.
The beginning of the end is beginning to take place.
This is no time for regrets however, so none will come from my face.
I always felt like a dolphin that was brave but lost at sea.
And I don't think that creation had intended that for me.
It is human nature to take for granted the things we think we are owed.
Unfortunately that thinking ends up becoming a lonely, one lane road.
This is the end of my journey, at least with the familiar face I have been wearing.
I would like to thank everyone for my farewell, thank you all for caring.
I think I have done a pretty good job of making sense of it all.
We are all leaves on one tree, anticipating the first chill of a fall.
The gates are opening now and the warmth of safety is running through my soul.
Remember that death is not the end, so do not let it stop you from your goal.

To Jimmy

Summer, 2003

You know, there are some angry and broken hearted people down here, stuck in the wake you have left.

It feels as if God is some sort of life robber and you were simply his theft.

No mother should ever have to say goodbye to a son, whose life expired way too soon.

And the only solace she now has are memories and an upward look towards the fading moon.

I cannot imagine how much you must have suffered at times, wrestling with your mortal thoughts.

Trying to master the knowledge of what you understood, while attempting to understand your faults.

But like the sun, you have set down to rest far too soon. It just never seems right.

There are no answers to our questions or no comfort in the dawns early light.

It is a tragedy that does not need to be explained, just mourned until it hurts no more.

And it just doesn't do any good to try to understand another person's inner war.

In the end, we all must face our demons. We will all try to make sense of our lives down here.

It is preparation for the possible futures in heaven, when we can once again hold each other near.

And laugh about the hell we raised on earth, or the simple moments we took for granted.

When we thought we were permanent fixtures and would never perish, we were trees that were firmly planted.

But those memories are what gets us through the teary eyed pain of mortality and sorrow.

And even though I may not see you again for some time, I will continue to think of you tomorrow.

To My Teacher

Fall, 2005

"Lights, camera, action" represents more than just a saying. It represents to me a way of life.

It's how you wake up in the morning, go about your daily duties, talk to friends and kiss your wife.

Only one man can go about his life with as much gusto as the one who left us far behind.

The rest of us are just impersonators with dedication and imagination, only in our minds.

I will always remember the word, "cut" in my life. It was a culmination of achievements and endings all in one.

The relief of the bright lights going off from up above and the pride of a job well done.

We would try to wrap up early during those days, simply in hopes of hearing more stories of life from a seasoned vet.

His action and adventure would spew out while the eager kids would, on the storyteller hedge their bets.

In a sense he was more than just a director of a show. He was a mentor, a leader and an advice giver.

Ten years later his direction continues to flow through my life like that of the deepest river.

How many of us will be able to say we died doing something we enjoyed? How many of us even do the things we actually enjoy?

Mr. H always did. And I get the sneaking suspicion that what we saw and heard was so much more than just a ploy.

The body may have left this earth, but thank heaven the memories will always remain.

They are the only tangible things we can hold onto. Without them, life would drive us all insane.

It is perhaps too late to thank him myself for a job well done, so I will say it in a written remark.

The bright lights have finally gone off after a job well done but the studio has prematurely fallen dark.

Goodbye to a Friend

Fall, 2004

It is hard to see the happy events that are in the distance, when our vision is blurred with teary eyes.

I used to awaken in the middle of the night to see her in the window, now I must look to the skies.

She is everywhere all the time and yet neither of us can touch her fur or kiss her head.

And even though we watched her pass from this life to the next, it feels as if all of us are dead.

All we have are cold hard picture frames with her face to look into, or a memory that is burned with death.

I couldn't even seem to utter a coherent sound from my sorrowful voice when I watched her take her final breath.

I know that the lumps in our throats and the cracks in our hearts will subside, but I wish I knew when.

All we have left are desires to move on through this life with the eventual hope of seeing her again.

We just hope that she is looking down at us with joy, because we are looking up at her with pain.

We feel as if we are teetering between the things that make us whole and things that are driving us insane.

I know I have my wife who can hold onto me while I hold tightly onto her, pushing through the initial blast.

But a life that ends only after eight short years is a life that in my eyes ends too fast.

And so with that I would like to say goodbye to the joyful ten pound bag of fur that made the most serious of problems disappear.

And if we are no longer able to hold onto you, at least we can hold your memories and your pictures near.

Auditorium

Fall, 2004

The attendees gather in the auditorium this morning, dressed in the clothes they wore the day before.

Many of them are so preoccupied with the idea of being here that they simply don't care about fashion anymore.

People from all over God's creation have arrived for the in depth orientation that takes place each and every morning.

Some have been eagerly awaiting the gathering, while others have arrived here without warning.

One arrived late, still holding onto the empty bottle he was nursing while driving on the rain slicked interstate.

He is joined by the coma patient who waited at the entrance for years, happily reaching her departure date.

The first presenter at the show welcomes everyone to the auditorium and asks that they take a seat.

Just as a drug addicted prostitute and an AIDS victim help a tired old lady off of her feet.

The presenter begins with a prayer and a whisper to the loved ones who have come through here before.

He then proclaims, "I hope you all have left your Religion and empty faith at the auditorium door?"

It is at that moment that hundreds realize for the first time where they are.

It makes perfect sense to the depressed soul with the wrists' full of scars.

Or the victim of a hit and run, who hung on long enough to tell his family goodbye.

This is the waiting room for Heaven, the first place you enter when you die.

It's a nice thought that we as a people may finally reach a place where hate is left at the auditorium door.

But it is just too bad that we have to wait that long to understand what life should really be lived for.

Heaven

Spring, 2004

I hope that when I get into Heaven I will have an ocean front room with a beautiful view.

I want to see the sands, rich with a golden tan and the ocean, an intoxicating blue.

Hopefully it will be a place in which I can sit on the balcony, breathing in the salty air.

And unlike the days of life, I can sit around and let time pass by with hardly a care.

It will be a place where the ocean is always warm and the sun is always strong.

It is where the scent of my wife will remain on my breath and the dance will always be long.

In my mind Heaven will be a place where my family is right down the hall.

And my friends will be around to pick up the phone when I give them a call.

There will be no such things as alarm clocks going off in the early hours of the day.

No reckless drivers buzzing by you with a finger in the air, yelling "get out of my way!"

Paradise will be a place where my insecurities get swept away with the salty waves.

It is where I don't need to see the warnings that "Shit happens" or "Jesus saves."

Perhaps even goals that were told to me that needed to be achieved in life will not matter in the least.

It is where we don't have to fight and claw for food and drink because every day will be a feast.

And every evening dinner will be reserved at a five star café, with desserts being carted out for every craving.

There will be no need for bank tellers or mortgage lenders because there will be no need for saving.

And a midday nap can be as long as you please. You won't need to be awoken for anything special you might miss.

It is where a paycheck is non existent and a handshake is not nearly as important as a kiss.

And the sky is crystal blue to match the sea and the clouds are a puffy, marshmallow white.

Not the depressing, rain producing gray that I am sure to see tonight.

Age

Fall, 2003

I do know that one day I will be in a chair speaking to a relative of mine, who isn't even born.
Of what it is like having more days behind then ahead, feeling tired, old and worn.
"It is both a blessing and a curse to grow old," I will tell them. "Not everyone gets the chance.
They spend all their time waiting for the musician to sing a sweeter tune that they forget to dance."
And before you know it, fifty years have passed in hurried breaths and angered tones.
Instead of being the focal point of your family, you are left waiting for ringing phones.
One meager check is the gift to the elderly for all those years of dedicated service.
And the simple fact that one day I will be in that position is already making me feel nervous.
Perhaps I will have to decide which pills are more important for the extension of my days.
I will make the preparations for the family, when we go our separate ways.
I will pawn off my worldly possessions which were just pointless collections of my youth.
Throwing my legacy over the side of a bridge can be more painful than the truth.
Understanding that the day of my birth is a memory not even had by me.
What is really sad is that my death will be up there for everyone I won't know to see.
They will get up to the podium, speaking through tears and unsteady voices.
Of all the trials and tribulations I endured, of all the brilliant choices.
But who are they to tell the masses what I was all about?
They were only wombs or ideas when I was looking for my route.
When I was truly alive and full of life, I was getting to know the elders ahead of me.
Now I find myself being introduced to the youthful children on my knee.
I guess what makes the world go round, is that everyone gets their chance.
It's just that some people choose to sit and watch, while others choose to dance.
So before the fears or acceptance of age begin to creep in on my time here,
I should take a look at what I have today and forget about the future that is near.

Sandy Beach

Winter, 2004

I hold my Grandmother's elderly hand in the morning and in the evening my Grandson may hold mine.

Together we peer into mirrors that echo wisdom and experience all the way down the proverbial line.

Wedged in between old and new, we witness everything and nothing at the very same time.

We sing the end of some verses and the beginning of others, but the songs don't seem to rhyme.

There seems to be an abundance of people to comfort us through sorrow, but no one that can quite relate.

And on this road to nowhere we find ourselves on, it is either by a simple act of coincidence or fate.

Maybe before it's all over with I will find myself running over a sandy beach, towards the oceans shore.

I will watch the high flying kites of my yesterdays, struggling and yearning for a little more.

Perhaps when I get to the shore, I will find a piece of seaweed to use as a mustache on my face.

And I too can parade around like a pirate, making children laugh in this remote vacation place.

That will be my goodbye to someone who would have wanted to do the very same,

But who has run out of opportunities to watch the setting sun, having to forfeit the game.

The fact remains that there is always someone heading out while another may be heading in.

What has to end for someone who gave their all for life, is allowing another one to begin.

Passing
Winter, 2004

And the generations pass, like the blink of an eye.

Memories are lost and found in between a laugh and a cry.

Older eyes peering out into the open sea of mortality's wishing well.

Fishing for the hands of the past to reach out, carrying a story to tell.

While other eyes are opening for the very first time, innocence covered by blue.

We say goodbye to a great grandmother who is almost ready to pass on through.

We start out young, with no idea of the roads that may lie ahead.

And some of us end up young again, with no idea of what is in our heads.

Others don't even get the chance to see thirty six, tragedy at every door.

At what point is it okay to put down the sword and say, "I don't need this anymore?"

It is almost like each new day is an unknown challenge, a life or death existence.

And the hardest thing about making it to bed every night is the constant struggle between submission and resistance.

And so we pass the baton to loved ones we will never see, hope is all we hold.

Relying on fading memories of previous loved ones and the stories they have told.

It may be that we are destined to advance only to a certain time. Luck is a breeze that does not refresh us all.

But at least we have the comfort in knowing that generations pass like the end of summer to the beginning of fall.

In a Field of Wheat

Summer, 2005

I begin to feel the first soft rain drops from a cloudy sky, falling gently on my face.
I still concentrate on the impending hills in front of me, continuing to walk at a medium pace.
The sun is getting ready to settle in behind this hazy shade of grey.
And like most things in my life, I miss them most right before they go away.
If this desolate field that I am walking is never ending, then I will fall well short of all my goals.
And each little storm cloud that comes over my head will greedily take its toll.
No one wants to think of their journey as barren and cold, life is better when the heart is warm.
But sometimes, no matter how frequently you swat at the silly ideas in your mind, they still swarm.
This is not a testament to the power of the mind, rather to the ignorance of our thoughts.
We could do ninety eight things correctly out of one hundred and we are still remembered for our faults.
Some of us walk through each day with a sense of defiance and remorse, not listening to what is said.
And I would play high stakes poker with my emotions if I could just get them out of my head.
There is a rush to accomplish everything you can before you finally clock out and head home.
And while some of us have it all down in an organized manner, most of us just roam.
So here I am in this field of wheat and clouds, roaming around looking for pieces to my map.
I have ideas of finding everything before the rains start to come, but it would be so nice to take a nap.
And the last bus is getting ready to pull out of the station, how I hate being left behind.
But there are so many things I am still in search of and they are things I really need to find.

Swirls
Fall, 2004

Did I just see what I wanted to see, or was it just a dream in another long night?
Because I could have sworn I had an image when absolutely everything turned out alright.
I love the ice cream swirls inside my mind, making up for summers long since passed.
The little innocent girls would chase us boys around for no other reason but to harass.
Those summer days seemed to last forever, before mom yelled that it was time for bed.
But the images that were there in the moments have been burned into my head.
And when I think about the little person growing inside my wife, I automatically smile.
Because I am sure they will experience the same things I did in previous miles.
Perhaps it will be my turn to yell at my kids, "Are you trying to cool the rest of the neighborhood?
Because if you are, than the job you are doing is so very good!"
The ice cream trucks and kick ball games will mix with the humid August days.
And the neighborhood legend award is given to you when you make those game saving plays.
Life seems to last forever under the humid summer sun, nothing you touch goes wrong.
And with the thought of winter in the back of your mind, you wonder if that will be as long.
And when it comes you adjust, because in life that is all that you can really do.
Because the seasonal memories you create never leave when they are through.

A Leaf

Spring, 2005

Yesterday must have been a rotten day to be a leaf, held captive by the wicked winter winds.

It just moved at the mercy of its own weakness, no means performed, just more pointless ends.

Six months after his last friend fell off a tree and died, he floats in between life and certain death.

He is unable to formulate a cohesive thought and he lacks the ability to catch his tired breath.

He's cascaded over footpaths and into rippled creeks, still cold with winter frost.

Passing over young lovers anticipating the first spring breeze, hoping to recapture what was lost.

Bounding aimlessly into trees and bushes like a clumsy man who had a few too many.

He rolls over pavement cracks that break your mothers back and a face down penny.

Eventually finding a wide open door to an old antique store, he enters to take a rest.

He winds up decomposing in the store with the rest of the junk that couldn't pass the test.

So we all gather in life to float for awhile, skimming over experiences as they pass us by.

Hoping to experience all we desire before the day comes for us to wither away and die.

But before that moment of closure, take today to walk outside and smell that sweet spring air.

Because today is an absolutely wonderful day to be a leaf and most of us just don't care.

Shaking Wildly

Fall, 1998

The leaves shake wildly in the wind, trying everything to hold onto their trees.
Old man winters around the corner, blatantly ignoring their desperate pleas.
The last of the insects are fighting the impossible task of trying to stay alive.
It was just a few months earlier when all of them had thrived.
Clouds are looking a bit more ominous to the weary traveler. A hard cold is on its way.
The first hint of burning firewood is in the air today.
If I could cry a thousand tears, it would not put the salt back into the sea.
The indefinite feeling of insecurity is the feeling that sticks with me.
You cannot climb a tree to hide from fear because the tree will be destroyed in time.
And the words I try to organize cannot have an impact, even if they rhyme.
We are birds of a feather, flocking together only when it suits our needs.
We carelessly cut down beautiful flowers so that we can exterminate the weeds.
The naked tree branches from far off trees are smacking unforgiving cries at the windows.
But the messages are not getting through to anyone, no one even knows.
The outside world is speeding by with no regards for what is going on behind closed doors.
We see only what we understand. The rest is just another person's chore.
With the overcoming sense of fear, the man sits alone on the cold park bench.
In his sabotage of life, he was both the monkey and the wrench.
The leaves have shed their caregiver's branches and now lay desperate on the ground.
They blow gently in the wind making a murmur but no one is there to hear the sound.

Superhero Without a Cape

Spring, 2005

There is a temporary void in my self that lets me down when the excitement leaves.

I imagine a magician, who no longer has anymore tricks to pull out of his sleeve.

Perhaps the cave is darkest when it is lit the fullest, it's just the anticipation of the conclusion.

And all the roller coaster experiences we share with each other, by the end are just illusions.

Life altering events go by the fastest, so fast you aren't even aware they are life altering.

And people only seem interested in your accomplishments when you are dead or faltering.

I understand that loneliness is simply a state of mind and a state of mind is boredom gone berserk.

It just seems ironic that the hardest type of "lonely" is the one you knew would never work.

I feel like a superhero that misplaced his cape but couldn't even fly when he had it on.

But if the past holds true I know I will feel better when the new day displays it dawn.

It is just that pit that never leaves. It only recedes when I don't need to watch myself collapse.

And will I ever seem to find reprieve from my sentimentality? Well probably not, but perhaps.

Bottom Line
Winter, 2005

I am but a whisper in a collective scream, my voice only carries inside my mind.
I search the madness for an explanation and more madness is all that I find.
The same face in the mirror greets me everyday and everyday I am tired.
I am the employer and the employee on these days and on these days I am fired.

Times sure are moving for us aren't they my friend?
We seem bound by decisions we cannot comprehend.
And yet, we understand the gravity of the situation as we age.
Another lost opportunity for redemption because fate has turned its page.

It is nothing more than something I don't have and it will never be obtained.
Because in my life all I seek is to get by and to be slightly entertained.

Saying Goodbye
Spring, 2004

I don't think I can pick you up on this one. The anger has engulfed your bleeding heart.
And no matter how hard I try to pull you out of the drowning pool, the piranhas have already been ripped apart.
Normally, I would have defended you first on any topic that could have ever been presented.
But those very same actions that got me praise back then only now are leaving me resented.
And if I could tolerate your hatred for anything or anyone that makes me happy, I would really try.
But the things on the horizon in my life are making me ecstatic and with that I need to say goodbye.
We simply went down different paths after experiencing similar situations.
You prefer to cover up the past with righteousness, Religion and a ton of hesitation.
You reenergize the belief in your mind that the problems are inside of everyone else.
Never being able to take the hit to your ego, you blame everyone but yourself.
You always make me out to be the bad guy, upset that you were not the first one to learn.
Your anger keeps you warm at night while I sit in the distance, safe from the scorn
I understand that you got jealous when the spotlight was finally being held by another.
But perhaps you needed to take a look in the mirror and understand that it was your father or your sister or your brother.
I was protected by something bigger. Perhaps it was the warmth and comfort of understanding.
The fact that others can pick me up when I fall down makes my life seem less demanding.
I don't think you expected me to simply drop out of the race being run inside your mind.
But I cannot be competitive with someone whose heart I cannot seem to find.
And if this makes me the bad guy then so be it. I seem to have a knack for giving up.
I just cannot bring myself to drink the juice when I know there is only poison in the cup.

Ruthless Choices

Spring, 2004

A life that is full of failed promises and ruthless choices, seen in the eyes of a blinded soul.

Who, much like a snowball, gets up its momentum and then cannot stop its roll.

The witch hunt begins in earnest, searching for everyone who is deemed to have done you wrong.

And initially the list starts out very small, until the dedication of your anger makes it long.

Before you know it, family members and loved ones are up there on the chopping block.

They eagerly await execution or a pardon from the warden, before the last tick of the clock.

Moments of clarity are too few and far between, swirling confusion always interrupts.

Funny how the time spent on drama and petty disagreements can so righteously corrupt.

I know too many people who hold the book of God in one hand and a loaded gun in the other.

And when attempts at conversion fail, the gun gets pointed at an uncle, or a father or a brother.

But those bullets that you threaten to fire cannot pierce our skin, for it has grown too thick.

And the words that are shrouded in anger and frustration that once hurt, no longer have the ability to stick.

Tomorrow I plan on flapping my wings, ascending all the storm clouds that seem intent on staying.

I just hope you don't spend too much time on bended knee, reading passages and praying.

And when I get to the Garden of Eden one day, my route will have been different, but the end result the same.

It is far too easy in life to get wrapped up in competition that we all lose. What we seek is a place, not a game.

APB for Lady Luck

Winter, 2004

For right now the light at the end of the tunnel is being turned off. I prefer it dark.

And I couldn't remain with the pot of gold at the end of the rainbow. There wasn't any place to park.

I spent hours looking for the silver lining on every cloud that passed me by. But all I got was a bad neck ache and no answer to my only question. Why?

I fear what my fortune cookie will tell me today, lately they haven't been too kind.

And I had to put out an A.P.B. for lady luck, although I am afraid with what I'll find.

I tried to find a new leaf to turn over the other day, but unfortunately they have all been raked.

And my sarcastic optimism when I found the face down penny on the street was obviously faked.

The glass that used to be half full is now mostly empty, and besides that the water isn't even cold.

Even the words on my lottery ticket spelled out "pessimism." When did this world get so bold?

I am one tenth Irish but even that doesn't make a difference. The Leprechaun left long ago.

He mentioned that the only green I proudly display is envy and so he had to go.

Not even my cat had nine lives. If she did they were all used up on a Sunday night.

And could you please tell that damn electrician to turn off my tunnel light?!

Always, Never the Same (To a Friend)
Summer, 2002

The time bomb is ticking in my head tonight, capable of going off at anytime.
If I am truly a monster as people have said, than that is my only crime.
I wanted to be able to laugh when it suited me and I wanted to open up and cry.
But all I do is get red in the face with embarrassment and run away, wondering why.
Perhaps my parents coddled me to much? Talk about your rotten deals.
Thirty some years after my birth, they still insist on making all of my meals.
I would love to meet a woman to grow old with, but all I have is the thought of it.
When a man falls down and cannot get up, he eventually grows comfortable in his pit.
So now I just sit here on this hard twin bed, my parents sleeping quietly down the hall.
Either never realizing my potential or simply waiting again for me to fall.
I guess it doesn't really matter anymore. No one will miss me when I am finally gone.
No matter what is done in front of the moon, you are always forgiven by the light of the dawn.
So I will sit up and wait for a few more minutes before preparing to face another day.
They all start out and ultimately end, the same excruciating way.
It is a failure to meet my own personal goals, and a failure to even care.
One day soon however, a change will be coming. I can feel it in the air.
In the meantime, I will continue to get laughed at for my lack of "people skills."
I have one more day of sucking it up no matter what, even if it kills.
I will go about my daily routine no matter how mundane it may appear.
Because hope will always spring eternal, no matter how much in my life I may fear.

Ice Cream Swirl

Summer, 2003

I always hoped we would meet up again, at a vague corner store on the other side of a tired world.

It is where the flavors of our own experiences would coalesce to make the perfect ice cream swirl.

I think it is the place where hopes and dreams come together to make living a worthwhile proposition.

But so far the journey has only left me with a cynical remorse and a painful disposition.

I was misunderstood in my belief that life was all about the journey and not the final destination.

I now seem to be content with the idea that euphoria and companionship only leads to hesitation.

When you are young you have no use for the concept of time or the belief that the world is abstract.

You only needed to concern yourself with prepositional phrases and the ability to add and subtract.

As you get older you begin to realize that there is more to life than what you have been told.

And that you better do these things now before you grow comfortable in getting old.

And after the crazy ideas and reunions are planned, you realize no one else is thinking like that anymore.

So if you plan on walking any further, you better prepare to be completely alone as you open that door.

Because when you do, there will be no one left to wish you well or to throw encouragement your way.

And there in lies the dilemma. Do I take another chance all by myself or out of fear do I simply stay?

And so we go back to that perfect corner store picture that we painted all those years ago.

It is where the warm summer nights and the perfect ice creams swirls of kept innocence will go.

Never Mind

Summer, 1999

Never mind what has been said in the past or what will be said in the days
ahead.
Let us have this moment in time to concentrate only on what is currently being
said.
We both know that time will begin to tick and this moment will soon come to
pass.
And the shooting stars above will be making way for the morning dew on the
summer grass.
By the time the sun is strong tomorrow, you will be on a plane heading away.
So here I stand in constant wonderment, wishing I had the ability to extend
today.
The crickets are in the background again, like the first night we had met.
They sing sweet melodies within our heads, that we won't soon forget.
The full moon is directly above us, shining proudly for his moment in the sun.
Arrogantly expressing his misuse of time, like a prize is what he has won.
Pin that little ribbon on his chest if it makes him feel a little stronger.
As long as he is preoccupied you can stay a little longer.
It won't do any good I suppose. You are halfway home and the rest is leaving
fast.
Pretty soon all I will have of our time together will be painfully placed inside
the past.
It does no good for me to grieve for long. It never changes the end result.
And I cannot apologize for driving you away. It never was my fault.

Crossroads

Winter, 1998

I am standing at a crossroads with the stars in the sky,
While my conscience and I wonder why.
It is cold. Damn cold. My hands are becoming numb.
The truck that just passed must not have seen my hitched thumb.
These tears in my eyes laugh as they fall,
At the man they see, not giving his all.
With each step I take, pain shoots through my back.
Like soldiers in the bushes beyond, they just wait to attack.
The crossroads are here in my mind so that I may choose.
And at this very moment, I cannot afford to lose.
Do I turn and head back to the life that I had?
Where safety and security became corrupted and sad?
Or do I go straight where a new life can be found?
I want to find my goal of serenity, become safe and sound.
With my left hand in my pocket and the right one on my face,
Neither of us can seem to get familiar with the place.
I choose to go straight into a life that isn't clear.
I will come across another crossroads in a different time of year.

Wine and Roses

Summer, 2005

The days of wine and roses are better left behind us, fore beleaguered souls can't run.

The marathon for the rest of us began hours ago. You just never heard the starting gun.

It's funny in a way because we were always sort of running a bit behind the times.

We were like two children carelessly coloring blank pages, unable to stay within the lines.

In a way the last decade was a tale of attrition and disappointment, victories few and far between.

The introspective talking to the blank canvas before painting, I still doubt you know what I mean.

A man can carry innocence on his back for so long, eventually the weight becomes too much to bear.

But we can always carry tales of misadventure and boredom, sharing beer bellies and receding hair.

All chapters must end at some point however. No one is immune to growing up and eventually apart.

What may seem like an ending to some who wallow in sorrow is to others, simply another start.

The carousel can only spin so long before others find a horse and hop on board.

And with the nine lives I have expended already, how many more times can I fall on my sword?

So yes, I feel as if this is a final curtain call, an encore to a time when innocence was absolute.

It was where the consequences of shunning responsibilities were always accompanied by chocolates and a flute.

The sun has set on a chapter in my life I really don't care to revisit through a live mans eye.

This rebirth is another grand start in which something valuable to me in a moment, had to die.

Reminiscent

Spring, 2001

One way haze for a moment of smiles makes and breaks your heart in the same swift move,
While familiar faces sway carelessly with the out of tune singers, also trying to find a groove.
And then that moment passes and you are left waiting and wondering if another will present itself.
It is the fear that you will be doomed to live four more hours as a rusted out trophy on someone else's shelf.
You scan the room looking for the lonely familiar face with which you recently became acquainted.
And realize that even an angelic smile after awhile can become flawed and slightly tainted.
Flawed by no action of hers but rather by the way in which the world is viewed by you.
You damn all good natured things to hell because you couldn't hold a candle to what is true.
And then the music picks up and you drown yourself in memories of failure and despair.
You look around the room at old friends who are around, but were never really there.
And at this point you figure it is best to find your car and begin the long trip south.
You almost incidentally bring yourself to the level of others with that tired old mouth.
But you see her one more time in a hazy vision inside your head and decide to turn back.
Too bad for you the party is over, the guests are gone and the lights have faded to black.
And the car radio plays out something soft and melodic, almost miserable and slow.
Some years ago you could sing along and relate, but these days I'm not so sure you know.

One Last Bag

Summer, 2004

I packed my last bag today through tears and frustration of pain and relief.

Four of the five stages have long since come and gone, acceptance now replaces grief.

Of course this is all proverbial, fore I am quite settled into my life and rather happy for it.

I just got tired of being fatigued by the actions of others, having to put up with all of their sarcastic wit.

I have heard that life is broken up into different stages and passing one should be a goal.

But walking into each new chapter with a boulder growing larger, took too much of a toll.

And "fight vs. flight" became a running joke. Neither one could ever truly be obtained.

And ironically my emotions would be the one thing that could never be contained.

Like Dorothy on the yellow brick road, I needed to decide which way to proceed.

Should I turn around to the disrespect and malevolence or head towards what I want and what I need?

The decision wasn't nearly as tough as I made it out to be. My life was finally in my hands.

I have walked through the fires and rainstorms to find the beaches of peace and sands.

The fact is that no matter what, I will run to the aid of anyone I know. That is me.

But I cannot allow myself the confusion of what I am versus what others would like me to be.

So we get back to the bags that are packed, neatly in my mind. Emotional separation has concluded.

If blood is thicker than water, then can someone please tell me why both have become diluted?

I think I have decided to fight for what I want and the flight is for anything unwelcome to my heart.

With the idea that every ending in life except for one, is another exciting and unknown start.

And if people would like to be there with me, my auditorium doors will always be open.

But I won't be pacing nervously back and forth, praying for a return of one, or endlessly hoping.

Lies
Winter, 2000

The lies reverberated off of your lips with an almost simplistic beauty and ease.

As you tried everything you could to wrap me around your finger and bring me to my knees.

It must have felt for a moment as if you were succeeding fore I played the part so well.

I pretended to be vulnerable as I compared potential loneliness with hell.

The way I looked distraught, the fear must have really shown inside my eyes.

Like my whole life was like a race and you were the red ribbon prize.

I remember telling you how I felt as I made bold predictions along the way.

I made mock guarantees in hypothetical hopes that you would stay.

Mostly doing all of this in hopes of easing my own descent, knowing I fall too fast.

I made contingency plans for my heart in case your kind deception did not last.

I knew there was a chance that eventually true colors would be painted.

And that the words spewing from your mouth would become quite tainted.

Not brought on by insecurity of my past, but of my insecurity towards you.

I understood that if I continued to fall, my heart would grow sour and blue.

I guess it was ultimately a game that we ended up playing and I always play to win.

So that my friend is honesty and a lot of honesty in our world was based in sin.

I cannot tell you how to tell me what you feel nor can I pretend I did not care.

But the thought of you being with someone as coy as you, is a thought I cannot bear.

I admired your apparent honesty despite the fact that I never saw it released.

And once I lost trust in your believability, my cooperation ceased.

I do wish you the best of luck. I hope one day that you can stand up tall.

But if one day you realize that you made a mistake with me, do not try to call.

Hope Springs Eternal

Spring, 2004

You drag yourself into your security blanket. It is the only place in which you still feel warm.

The medication is quickly numbing the bees in your mind that were getting ready to swarm.

Everything is safe for now. You are at peace with your ringing mind.

Even your heart beats in joy, despite the love you have been unable to find.

The day that started out so bleak has become your greatest day of all.

No one was on alert to catch you because there was no chance that you would fall.

But as the day becomes the evening and the sun is setting to the west,

Your harmonic sleep is interrupted by the demons who know you best.

The peaceful dreams of an ocean breeze are stopped by the storms from overhead.

The waves crash violently now and all the ocean life is dead.

The voices that were muted before are once again yelling into your ear.

Requesting that you join them once again, they will fight your fear.

You spring awake from these nightly visions with tears running down your face.

You look to the heavens in frustration, wishing that God would wipe you from this place.

There is no more medication in sight for you this evening. There are no more pills to take.

Only an empty slate of unfulfilled promises and a journey you must make.

The road will be a lonely one at first, but you must persevere through all the haze.

Forget about the paths chosen in the past, focus on the better days.

The choice is up to you right now, in the cricket chirping evening you have known.

I hope this moment is the opportunity for you to display the potential you have shown.

But you drag yourself back into your security blanket. It is the only place in which you still feel warm.

The medication is quickly numbing the bees in your mind that were getting ready to swarm.

Perhaps tomorrow will mark your emergence from this motley cycle in which you spin.

Because only you have the ability to get out of this quagmire you are in.

Walking

Summer, 1999

I am perfectly content with the path I have been walking.
And you still do not understand why we had to stop talking.
I didn't want to walk hand in hand on some empty, windy beach.
Or touch your chest to make sure that your heart still beats.
It wasn't enough that you were the only one to care.
Love was never something that we mutually shared.
You could not compete with a ghost from my past.
When I rested my eyes it was her I saw last.
So here I am on a one man path.
I have no one to hold. Now you do the math.
I have often thought that if grass is greener on the other side.
Is love like a rollercoaster that we all must ride?
Is it better to be lonely, or just simply alone?
You cannot wait for the ring if you have turned off your phone.
I am perfectly content with the path I have been walking.
And you still do not understand why we had to stop talking.

These Days
Summer, 2004

They say that it's best to simply let things go, to let them in one ear and out the other.

Some of us prefer standing up to the fire, while others will undoubtedly run for cover.

It sure is easy to take a good hard look at oneself in the mirror, and be disgusted by what you see.

It is another to look past the wrinkles or extra pounds and say, "hey, no matter what, this is me."

Human nature can be the cruelest form of torture this world has ever seen.

And only when you truly experience the ignorance of others will you know what I mean.

It is a shame that we live in a time when it has become acceptable to label other people.

We no longer use a knife to stab someone in the back. We use a church steeple.

Or anything else from God's arsenal or fate's cruel idea of what is just.

Half of our hearts have bled out completely, the others will just rust.

I hope one day we can find a common ground, where insults are put away.

But with each cruel tick of the fateful clock, opportunities are dying today.

I want to walk away from the cruel and wicked, but I don't want to be shot in the back.

I want you to judge me for all the qualities that I have and not for what I lack.

Isn't hope all we ever have anyway? At what point was that forgotten about?

Don't you get more with a complimentary whisper, than a vulgar, disgusting shout?

Bookstores

Spring, 2004

The self righteous line up outside of the bookstores today, buying into their own life stories.

Segregated speakers carefully focus only on certain ears, eliminating fear and other worries.

The only things mentioned are one sided stories in what would normally be a two story book.

But it is impossible to win the war of viewpoints when others are allowed to take a look.

Conformity only depends on the amount of soul in a given body of life.

And the two results stemming from the scenario are holding onto, or getting stabbed with the knife.

Black and white are the only two view points, gray is only produced from a rainy day.

So if you plan on buying into the supposed vacation they produce, you better put the umbrellas away.

It would appear as if bitterness and self righteousness walk together firmly with hand in hand.

But you better not peer over into the ocean of possibilities. Just focus your narrow minded eyes on the sand.

It is like watching the same scenario every day out of my second story window.

At some point the tree will need to be removed from my yard, so that its roots can begin to grow.

Just don't count on that happening anytime soon. Life can get very comfortable swimming in hate.

And if you think the words of guilt and conversion will work on me, just be prepared to wait.

I find that life is better served when screwing up is something that is always allowed to occur.

Each incident is simply an ingredient and each one of us should be encouraged to stir.

Havoc

Summer, 2005

There is a man who sits in his corner of the world, looking for signs of the apocalypse.

And between hurricanes and terrorist threats, he polishes his guns and sharpens his whips.

As the acronyms point fingers at each other over impending disasters, hell benders smile.

Simply at the fact that they didn't need to manufacture the havoc because it was within us all the while.

So you can die in a foreign country fighting a war that no one seems to be able to understand,

Or you can die in your flooded home, awaiting a welfare check that was always in demand.

You need not concern yourself with tomorrow anymore because today is hard enough to see.

And it's copasetic as long we don't ask the questions and we can "be all we can be."

It doesn't matter how much a gallon costs because we all continue to pump away.

While the price gougers behind the plate glass windows coyly smile and say, "Have a good day."

Let's watch the homeless and downtrodden swim in feces and human waste while the President visits Texaco.

It's like sitting in front of a television set watching a rerun of the country's least favorite show.

And back to that man who is expecting the world to end, I doubt he has that long to wait.

I sure get the impression that we are heading towards a dead end existence that is ripe with blind eyes and hate.

Perhaps everything up to this point is a simple mistake, coincidence or aberration?

It gives one plenty to think about when waiting in line for a five dollar gallon at the local gas station.

Clarity
Spring, 2002

If we were born with clarity and compassion than I doubt this world would be so tough.
The things we spend a lifetime complaining about are the things that we make rough.
While we are consumed with anger, our attention to understanding all but disappears.
And only as we enter the grave will we look back upon those wasted years.
All life is for someone is a culmination of moments, both grand and obsolete.
The fact that we recall them in obscure moments is what makes them seem so sweet.
Too bad that many people would rather look to the heavens to pick them up today.
When in fact the very saviors they are praying to, have put them here this way.
If we could only learn that the walk is more important than the final destination,
Then people would no longer fear the feeling that accompanies hesitation.
But we are here to bump our heads when our limitations are in question.
It is funny how we never seem to agree with rock solid answers, yet we always flock to a suggestion.
I hope one day this world will evolve beyond our own selfish thought.
And that day would mark the end to all the endless battles we have fought.
At this moment however, our insecurity is our lone best friend.
The dream of peace is right behind our lonely ideals. We just have no choice but to defend.

I Have To

Winter, 2005

I have to get on that bus today, make new plans for a big getaway.
Or walk a thousand miles just to make you want to stay.
I have to hop on that carousel and roll around until my head begins to spin.
Or scale a mountain faster than anyone so I can have a chance to win.
I have to run like I am running from the law, hide out until my memory fades.
Or bluff my way into a high stakes game of poker, pinochle or spades.
I have to get a new identity or a better perception of the one I've got.
Or at least feign ignorance to those around me before putting others on the spot.
I have to get a new hobby because it seems the ones I have are getting old.
Or at least pretend to be interested in what I do before I leave myself out in the cold.
I have to jump on a faster train tomorrow because the one I drive today is way to slow.
Or just stop complaining about the misadventures that are going on inside my show.
I have to write it down when it suits my pen, or cry when it suits my eyes.
Or begin to understand that honesty is sometimes a veil and behind it are more lies.
I have to get to a higher place and take the ones I love, with me for the ride.
Or at least get up enough courage to admit to others that I just want to hide.
I have to live before I have to die, lessons from a library book that can never be returned.
Or begin to cope with what I am before the fire in my heart leaves my body burned.
I have to get it all in before it is time to check out of this happy hotel.
Or at least learn to laugh when you laugh, and to laugh when you yell.

Learning to Learn
Summer, 2003

If life was a scoop of chocolate ice cream on a banana, floating ignorantly in the melt that it makes,

Then I am the spoon that wishes I was the straw in the middle of a strawberry vanilla shake.

I am a law abiding person with a conscience working hard to live another day.

So please put down your picket signs of disapproval, turn your backs and walk away.

Support for something I am trying to understand is not recommended. Hell, it isn't even needed.

If it is necessary for me to feel the loss before I can appreciate the victory, than let me feel defeated.

And if it becomes necessary for me to walk sleeplessly through another night of hollow questions,

Then I am doing that for a reason and the reason is not to gather a million people's suggestions.

Yes, it will probably become necessary for me to hit rock bottom before I can learn about the value of life.

And while I turn a corner every single day, somewhere in the back of my mind I still swim in my own strife.

I know without a shadow of a doubt that everything I need to accomplish in my life will be there for the taking.

It's just that sometimes in order to refocus on the goals at hand, I need those hands to continue shaking.

Those are reactions to the fear that things will be taken away from me in the last chapter of my book.

And the defeatist in me sees the irony of worrying about the last chapter when I haven't even started to look.

Therefore, how can I know the outcome of what isn't even written? I don't think I am even halfway done.

And even if I knew the fate of myself, I wouldn't go down without a fight and a glare towards the setting sun.

I have an awful lot of living left to do and I need to get it started. Life is too short to accept a fate that isn't even set.

And I don't approve of gambling but if you had to place an offer, then on me you should hedge your bet.

Two Sided Coin

Fall, 2005

I feel like I must go right or I must go left because straight is not an option anymore.
All my problems run parallel to each other and they hide behind each and every door.
It isn't enough to run from them these days, fore I am a bit older and a lot more slow.
I have tried hiding from what pains me the most but in reality there's just nowhere left to go.
There are no rocks to hide under in this desert, or no ladder that will carry me away.
If I don't face my fears tomorrow, I will live ten thousand more todays.

But that is just one side of this conflicting story. The other side has contentment and pleasure.
At twenty eight years old I have found the map, discovered the "X" and unburied my treasure.
So why add potential frustration to my life for something hypothetical that may never transpire?
Should my decisions be based on what I truly want, or by others who simply hold my feet to the fire?
Can a man be settled into his life when he hopes to have more days ahead than there are behind?
And is it better to just stop and live in the moment, or make contingency plans for things I may never find?

Is it better to plan for a trip that is a lifelong adventure, or to just enjoy each new day for what it brings?
I don't think it is possible to dance to the beat of a song while trying to listen to the verse that he sings
I just know that whatever I choose, I better be prepared to live without regret.
Because it seems to me that life doesn't stop when one person does, that's just the safest bet.

Journey
Winter, 2000

Journey with me friend on a path that has not been chosen by many,
Let me know what you fear, give me your thoughts for a penny.
Stop and wonder with me friend as I ponder a painful thought.
Help me to reinforce my understanding that lessons are learned and not bought.
Help me walk on the rocks of indecision as we climb the hills of fear.
And whisper thoughtful sentiments into my lonely, tired ear.
Decide with me the path to choose, when the road splits into three.
If I proceed right instead of going left, would you still proceed with me?
Would you point me out a star that had begun to lose its luster?
Or point me out another one that never did quite trust her?
Cry with me my friend, when the river of tears begins to flow.
Please teach my mind to assist my heart in learning to let go.
Help me to get to sleep when the fire has burned out.
And explain to me again what this journey is all about.

Openly Tired

Spring, 2005

The rain drops would fall like tears that were cried from the failing eyes of fate.
I feel like a lonely child with nothing but vegetables on my plate.
I waited for the approaching storm that is now coming into sight.
Apprehensive about the man I would become by the dawn of the morning's light.
Growing openly tired of walking along in this world as a single
I am apparently too strong to settle and arguably to weak to mingle.
I watch my face grow old in a mirror that gives me only the cold hard facts.
And knowing that if God had a hand, it would be my face he would smack.
I never wanted the keys to success on my chain if it sacrificed the simple pleasures.
But these days have become desperate times and therefore so have my measures.
Strong is just a word these days that means nothing to anyone who is not insecure.
That is because strength is found in men who are not afraid to open every door.
Certainties are for children to believe and guarantees are for people looking for hope.
Bees will sting and children will sing, but ignorance will always leave you hanging from the rope.
Would you rather trust a God that tells you to jump or a devil who does not agree?
When faith is really tested, will you believe in life or fall to a knee?
People can be blinded by how they feel and they become the lemmings, falling off of rocks.
Ideas are manufactured by your soul, not by the religious people riding around on bikes.
We can all be entitled to opinions and those opinions are what make us free.
They are always what we feel and understand, but not always what we see.

Patterns
Fall, 2004

We are all chasing time, trying to find where it is that we belong,
Before the musical chairs tune ends and we all stop singing along.
The weather is turning a little colder in our hearts these days,
And the once important fixtures in life will begin going their own ways.
Bigger and better challenges will await us, when spring breaks through next year.
We grow filled with concern and satisfaction as those interesting days grow near.
Life works like that though, as I have discovered through my writing.
All you need is a heart that bleeds, a pen that writes and a little bit of lightning.
And before you know it, the words of life have been recorded for all to see.
Verses that flow like a summer breeze have you singing on a bended knee.
And as the clocks turn farther and farther away from what we were,
We realize that the disease is terminal, and there is no cure.

A Walk
Summer, 2003

I saw a very old man in a wheelchair today and I decided to approach.
He was with some sort of assistant, perhaps a helper or a coach.
He looked me square in the face and said, "I wish I was still like you.
To be able to run and smile and accomplish with ease all you ever wanted to."
I fired back at him, "I wish I was like you are now, to know that I will be alive for a good long while.
To be able to know that I will have many years ahead, would allow me to endure each and every trial."

As I walked along a bit, I caught the eye of a little boy, looking up with curious questions.
I decided to approach him with a few tips and pointers, perhaps to give him some suggestions.
But when I got to him he whispered, "I wish I was like you. Fully grown and in charge of your path.
To be able to come and go as you please and to already have been educated in women, sports and math."
I knelt down and whispered to him, "I wish I was more like you, with unknown findings along the way.
The innocence and welcoming nature you still have, before things are learned and then fall in disarray."

The next person I noticed was a man, walking with his two little children. He seemed to be teaching.
I wanted to know what simple advice he was giving and if his parish was buying into the preaching.
He welcomed me in with a smile and said, "Enjoy the time before the children come, they will consume your life.
You will yearn for the days of peace and quiet, when you had the opportunity to spend time with just your wife."
I fired back, "I am envious of you as well. You have the opportunity to see your legacy carried down the line.
Nice to know that when you pass away, your memory will be carried and your family will be fine."

And then it hit me when I was left alone. Each face I saw was eventually my own.

Each character represented a piece of me that in the moment I must have wanted shown.

Everyone you meet is just an extension of yourself. That makes perfect sense to me.

There are no such things as strangers. You learn from what you want yourself to see.

Appreciation
Fall, 2002

The adults have a more weathered appearance these days. They exude wisdom from the accumulation of years.
They have seen an enormous amount of trials and tribulations. The have amassed additional tears.
With fewer days ahead of them than days behind, they enjoy the simple events going on around them everyday.
They are bidding fond farewells to life long friends who are constantly passing away.
They speak to the youth with knowledge and advice. They smile at our mistakes.
They understand the experience that comes with time and the patience that it takes.
It is almost as if they are unique history lessons, teaching from some old book.
They advise us to learn from our yesterdays, learning from them what it took.
They seem to be rushing to get it all in, squeezing it out before their own demise.
They appreciate the beauty of everyday events like a fresh sunrise.

The children see the elders' faces as merely mortal, like renters on this mistake ridden planet.
They only expect to see a million more tomorrows, a promotion and how to land it.
They ignore the words of the preachers and teachers, day dreaming of better things.
They listen only to the erupting beat of the songs and not the singer who poignantly sings.
They are paying no attention to the pleas of the older generations. They take what has been given to them for granted.
They choose only to eat the fruit provided on the vine as opposed to making sure another vine is planted.
Eventually, the years add up and they attempt to recapture that fading youth.
They ignore the receding hairlines and pot bellies, covering up the impending truth.
And before you know it the younger generation has become the older generation, with no guides or instructions kept.

And the last phase of a life is completely winged, as that is all that is left.

This cycle repeats itself as history comes full circle day in and day out.
We only realize the meaning of our lives when the circle comes about.
Perhaps we should stop to smell the roses when we are running over them at play.
And then we wouldn't have to squeeze it in when the completed circles come our way.

Routine Days

Summer, 2005

It is as if twenty seven years were a ticking clock that moved rapidly, like the blink of an eye.

We only seem to realize the finality of a situation when it is time to say goodbye.

Through the days and nights of our routine, we find comfort in the fact that we are here.

We take for granted that we have each other and more time in front of us, everything seems near.

But like the evening autumn sun, life is signaling a change that is coming at us fast.

And like a thief we try to steal the comfortable moments before they all go past.

Unfortunately there are far too many times we get lost in the haze of a routine day.

Like the sand on a summer beach, we watch helplessly as the tide takes us away.

But through the pain we are left with a gift of time and wisdom that can never be replaced.

A certain gratitude and appreciation for all the obstacles we have faced.

Character is not an actor in a play. It is what you gain from a life filled with hurdles.

Sometimes we must gallop through them like a horse while others we trudge through like turtles.

But with a big heart and a lot to give, you wake up and head out for your last routine day.

With admirers behind you and the rest of your life in front, you continue to live life your way.

Night
Fall, 2005

At some point in the evening, my rationality heads to the basement while my panic heads upstairs.

And despite the deadened night being lonely, I know the loved one next to me cares.

But the leaky faucet in my mind keeps dripping. No matter how hard I turn the valve it drips.

While the little doubting Thomas on my shoulder begs and pleads for me to take another sip.

And the tide in my stomach comes in high like the sea, dark and cold under the stars.

Eventually I begin to understand that the answer to my equation is anxiety, caused by scars.

Just as that startling revelation presents itself, I fade away into another night of sleep,

For a dream I can only vaguely remember by the new dawns light, a slippery mountain steep.

And the problem has escaped my mind, finding refuge in the excitement of a brand new day.

But just because it lies there dormant in the fresh morning hours, doesn't mean it went away.

The battle rages on, but I won't let go of your hand no matter how hot the fire gets.

Because he who lives to see the success of his own sweat is a man that never quits.

Life Cycle
Fall, 2004

You start out as an idea or an accident in the minds of others, but immediately things start taking place.

Bones and blood are forming rapidly; the first hints of skin are starting to form a face.

The delivery into the world is a distant thought at this point, contemplation is not a selection.

The only thing on your mind is the celestial fluid you are warming in; an ideal perfection.

All of a sudden the world you know is ending abruptly, the volcano is starting to erupt.

And while the delivery of her baby is excruciatingly long to Mom, to you it is abrupt.

The lights of an unknown world are spinning around to your under developed eyes.

And it is completely odd to you why people seem relieved by your uncomfortable cries.

But a year has passed in the blink of an eye; time is not something you can even comprehend.

At four you realize that two hours are never ending; eternity is always up around the bend.

When seven hits your first pet passes away and the knife you feel in your chest is betrayal. You have a feeling that it all will cease.

That what you have grown so comfortable in doing will eventually end and that it may not even be a sweet release.

At ten you begin to see the imperfections of parents and friends, violence and disappointments in all of their ugly forms.

Twelve reaches you and a crush feels like a renewal of spring. She is like a buzzing bee that is full of honey, she just never swarms.

Disappointment at thirteen comes in pubescent forms, questions swirl around your mind like a fire in the forest.

At fifteen, with an eye on the future and an ear towards the ladies; your grades are at their poorest.

By twenty you realize that answers may not be a possibility, life is just a fateful collection of decisions.

At twenty three you can begin to see the scar tissue on your soul, an accumulation of all the painful incisions.

But at twenty five the outlook is not so bleak; a girl you met has agreed to be your wife.

And at twenty seven you have settled comfortably into your new home and ultimately your new life.

Twenty eight brings a little daughter into the fold, full of questions she has not yet learned to ask.

But by thirty you will be taking your little mischievous love child to reprimand and task.

You lose your hair at forty, but gain introspection and wisdom at forty-five.

Puzzled as to why now, at fifty you may actually feel even more alive.

At sixty you begin to realize that the light is dimming a bit, but it still has years to burn.

When you climb the mountain to seventy you either accept the lesson or stubbornly realize you still have a lot to learn.

At eighty, with health hurdles overcome and your family out there learning on their own, death can be accepted.

But in the meantime, the appreciation is overwhelming when you realize that this life can still be perfected.

As ninety approaches and breathing grows shallow, family gathers to wish you a fond farewell.

And off in the distance somewhere, another idea is getting started. You just cannot hear the ringing of that conception bell.

Creaky Boat

Summer, 1999

Hope is like a boat in the middle of the sea.
My arms are like the paddles, straining to be free.
Unable to keep up with the better looking boats,
I just sit on creaky wood, hoping to stay afloat.
They are racing towards something, not yet seen,
While I am trying to enjoy the journey, making sense of what it all means.
The repercussions of the bigger boats waves' toss me upon the sea.
Leave it to others to not realize what their actions do to me.
It doesn't really matter now because the sun is getting ready to set.
I don't know what that does for others, but it makes me feel content.
I could just lie back in my boat and pray for falling stars
I hope that at least some of them have taken the journey to mars.
I do wonder where they fall. Do they just disappear into the sea?
If I could choose my own fate, that would be perfect for me.
How great would it be to be what everyone wishes upon?
To be responsible for everyone's hopes, to be that strongly counted on.
I just sit upon the sea with no set direction in my mind.
I have endless opportunities in front and bittersweet memories behind.

Eventually

Spring 2004

Eventually you will get well past the point of no return.
Where everything you try to touch begins to burn.
No matter how righteous and willing you may become.
You will undoubtedly be left out in the cold with an upward pointing thumb.
And an upward pointing nose at everything different in nature than you.
You spend all your time diagnosing us, finding out why we are blue.
For awhile we will try to chip away at the wall you stand in front of.
We will not do it out of stubbornness of frustration. We will do it out of love.
But eventually the last chipper will throw down his sword and walk away.
All along you had never intended for any of us to stay.
And the past you worked so hard to erase, will be put under a carpet in your new home.
The unborn children will not get to see the beliefs that you and yours condone.
And the ones you worked so hard to save will just have to find solutions by making mistakes.
Doesn't life reward the hardships of giving too much? I think that is what it takes.
You cannot save someone else when you cannot see the error in your demanding ways.
Nor can you move on through the inferno of a past you work so hard to lock away.
All along I just want everyone I care about to find the happiness I have discovered.
But when it comes to my personal belief in the good I can provide, I will keep it covered.

Walls
Winter, 2004

Four separate walls stand together in a semi-broken home. It is a home with a long, dramatic past.
One wall stands as a model for the other three. It stands somewhat damaged but always seems to last.
Its paint is somewhat faded and it has a couple of dents and warps, but it stands proud and it stands tall.
It only worries about living for each moment and is unconcerned with when it may crumble and fall.

The second wall has been there almost as long. It too has dents and bruises, but chooses to display them with pride.
It loves to tell anyone who will listen about the ups and downs of its wonderful ride.
It has its issues and some wear and tear, but overall it is proud of where it stands.
It uses abstract thoughts and the compassion of others to meet all of its demands.

The third wall has a beautiful portrait hanging on it, covering up anything that it does not want seen.
No one can have a true sense of what lies behind this portrait, good or bad or in between.
Like everything in life it has a story, but shame or anger prevents anyone from seeing its bruises.
This wall prevents anyone from truly getting to see its story and in return, we think it loses.

The fourth wall is the youngest of the group and it seems to be modeling itself exactly like the oldest.
Despite its emotional outbursts of colorful murals, it stands frightfully bare and is truly the coldest.
It is a relatively empty wall, waiting for someone to paint on its empty canvas, a beautiful scene.
The others walls hope it doesn't accept a tacky paint or one full of envy which is a deep dark green.

Each wall has a different way of coping with its weaknesses, each one displays its scars a different way.
Paint, wallpaper, portraits or an empty canvas tells of the character that we fight or accept and choose to display.

Let's Race

Summer, 2005

You are the sprinter at the starting gate, hoping the short burst will be your best.

I am the marathon runner just getting warm, eagerly awaiting my biggest test.

You seem hell bent on being first in every race you run even if the journey is a blur.

I just want to enjoy each passing tree or flower, the beauty of the race is what is pure.

You can label me a methodical loser or a lazy quitter. It makes no real difference to me.

I will just keep running my life like a marathon race, adjusting to everything I see.

Finish lines were created with the simple idea of labeling people as winners or losers.

It is a manufactured title for competitive knuckleheads and insecure abusers.

I have no time constraints on my life and I realize that. Because of this my race is never ending.

I will only slow down when my breathing has stopped and the Angels begin descending.

Until then I will keep on moving, taking nothing for granted except my healthy ability to keep on going.

I understand your desire to pass me by on anything. For you it is all about the mask of success that you are showing.

Long Before
Spring, 2004

Long before you could even remember, I was the shadow in your moments.
I worked diligently to smooth out the rough edges from those greedy opponents.
In the bowels of a darker side, I rowed through the places were hurt feelings are kept.
I tried to accommodate a broken heart that almost seemed comfortable with the way that it wept.
Emotionality was a weakness for some, but for you it must have been a curse.
In the great expanse of your mind I bet that honesty made it even worse.
And if excuses were the apples on an undiscovered apple tree, we would have nothing left to eat
Instead of dealing with a situation, it seems easier putting millions of miles underneath our feet.
I need to believe that somewhere in that journey our lives will begin to form a definition.
Or at the very least get a smile or a hug and just the slightest hint of recognition.
Optimism however is a gift for the young and innocence loses its luster after a while.
And it only takes a couple of beatings for even the most positive person to lose that smile.

Printed in the United States
48954LVS00005B/64-282

9 781424 134281